"I'd heard of the legendary mysterious Soulard Culture Squad but didn't really know what it was all about until Robert Boyd showed up at our Re: Born reading and graced us with a performance at the open mic. What style and mastery! He's been a regular now for some time and I'm so glad to see he's got a new book out, *A Fisher of Verses* (Spartan Press). Let's say he catches some big ones in this collection. If I had one word to describe the poems it would be: Unafraid. If I had several: Metaphorical, sensual, elegiac, amorous, wise. Here we see what happens to the still-radical: "agents/ and victims of a providence/beyond our power to know." And yet he does engage. He continues to question. Maybe what he's seen lends him the power to answer. Either way, you'll want to pick up this book and take part in the journey."

-Matthew Freeman, author of *Dopamine and the Devil* (Coffeetown Press), and co-curator of the Re: Born reading series in St Louis.

"In calling himself a "fisher of verses" Robert Boyd is being too modest. Caught in the many nets of his imagination are poems about his German ancestors that rival the best ever written, and lyrics that will transport readers back to their own honey-sweet moments of young love. Boyd is a well-published, prizewinning poet of love and its responsibilities, and this book presents us with his finest."

-Catherine Rankovic, author of *Meet Me: Writers in St. Louis*

A FISHER OF VERSES

Poems by Robert Boyd

Spartan Press

Spartan Press

Kansas City, Missouri

Copyright © Robert Boyd, 2026

First Edition: 1 3 5 7 9 10 8 6 4 2

ISBN: 979-8-89975-048-9

LCCN: 2026940060

Cover image: John Dean
Author photo: Katherine Boyd

Acknowledgments

Special thanks go to the editors of the following publi-cations where these poems first appeared:

"In the Orchard" appeared in *Chariton Review*

"Holding On in a Howling Wind," My Father Fishing," and "Uncle Herman, the Rake" appeared in *River Styx*

"C.B. Takes the Hand of Emma Ethyl Cook" appeared in *Nebo*

"My Son and a Friend on the Road in Texas" appeared in *Webster Review*

Table of Contents

SNAPSHOTS FROM MY FAMILY ALBUM

A FISHER OF VERSES

I spin out images like bright flies, tied
To lure the poems lurking in the pools . . .

When they strike they fight

But now and then I hook one
Reeling it wriggling and iridescent aloft
Gleaming and gasping in the unaccustomed air.

FOR KATHERINE, FOR LOVE

I am a boat on the sea of you

I rise when you lift me
And fall with your ebb

I spread myself like sail to catch your breath

Move me where you will.

FRAGMENTS TOWARD AN ELEGY

. . . in memory of JEB

Sometime this morning, by my German clock,
My little sister, half a world away, lay down to sleep
Her body wracked by medicine
Her spirit pacified with alcohol
And slipped through sleep into eternity.

From a tree whose leaves have almost gone
A flock of dark-winged birds, a few
Bursts forth and just as suddenly returns;
The scattered leaves, hung on the limbs
Like the Autumn's unused earrings,
Tremble, and a few more fall, in random swings,
And settle in the green October grass.

Off to the South the Alps rise, not quite visible;
Beneath the overcast, a thin slow rain.
And this is all I have, or shall, of her, whom after all
I scarcely knew, this image of a foreign place,
These lines, that bind some wisps of memory as they
    grow,
Thin but saving anchors to what's real and here:
The tree, its birds, its leaves, the grass, the dwindling
    year.

THE FIRST RAIN AFTER
A LONG, DRY SUMMER

Like syllables
Assembling
For a blessing

Like sweet birds
Alighting
In ones, fours, tens

After a long drought,
Cool and clean
And quickening,
The rain begins.

SPRING AGAIN

So there I am, inside the door
And glad, though not expecting it at all
She's left me in the parlor with its thick green rug
Shy, like an iceman asked in for a cigarette
Shifting my weight and whistling
With a scrap of brown leaf clinging to my heel

I'm sure she's coming on to me
What can I do but wait her out?
The wide room smells of secret parts
Like flowers, and the rug is soft as hair
The chaise is hollow where her thighs have been

Can't think of anything to say
Or where to move to, so I stand
And blush, getting a hard on, desperate
While she makes silken noises in another room.

NO ONE HANDLES FLOWERS
QUITE LIKE MABEL

No one handles flowers quite like Mabel
The butcher's girl
The one whose white breasts gap her blouse

Above the awning of her father's shop
She's lined the sill with tulips
Ferns crowd the corners of her living room
Her kitchen is alive with violets

Ah, from her bedroom we can hear her father's knife
Cutting a butcher's rhythm on red meat
To this beat she dances and unfolds
The petals of her own most secret rose
(And bites her lip
And calls me honey-bee.)

RED ROVER

In a dream I see you leaving from another room
I struggle to my feet but there you go
Before I reach you. You've cut your hair
Your eyes are darker now and deeper set
Still I'd know you anywhere.

The smell of lipstick starts this dream
Or fall of light through leaves
The slip of skirts on silken underthings
That evanescent hiss of women walking
It was the sound your hair made in my hands --

Back in my dream I hear you faint and far away
With other ghosts all in a line
Your laughter high and sweet
So from my distant side I cup my hands
And cry your name, and you look down
Unseeing, thinking of the wind, and then go on --
And in my dream I dream you running here with
    lovely strides
Your small feet whispering through the giving grass.

YOU HAVE TO BE A LOVER

You have to be a lover
Blind with the must of it
Pushing through chance to consequence
Kissing everything, one at a time --

You have to be a lover
Without bitterness without stinting
Like old sail bleached and thin
In the wind that scours
Hung out across the flow
Embracing change, engorging change
Hauling everything ahead --

O you have to be a lover.

**A LOVE SONG FOR THE SECOND
WEEK IN OCTOBER:**

Look the elm leaves lie in rings around the tree,
Lie where they've fallen, lie and do not move;
You cannot see the reason or the end of them.

There on the grass like lovers who don't move
Long after loving stops, they lie upon
Each other's thighs light in their Autumn bed
And dream of nothing, of no reason and no end
But lying loving in the nap of green
Still growing grass.

Look --
The yellow leaves, my love
Lie ringed around the bare black elm
That lifts its fingers to the empty air.

A LOVE SONG FOR MAY DAY

What a year for lilacs this has been
For hyacinths, for purple iris, all
Promiscuous, as louche
As rhododendrons, like long hair undone
Like just too much
Décolletage with hints of lace.

Imagine us running through fields of violets
Our bare feet amethyst with them
And falling down together in their
Blowsy swelling bosom
Our breaths fast and loose
And spicy with desire.

And afterward, imagine this:
I'll kiss your wine-sweet lips
Your cheek, the cleft between your breasts;
I'll make you lace of violets and bring
Lilacs by the armload, purple
And voluptuous for love
And pure white for surrender.

A LOVE SONG FOR THE ROAD FROM GIEN TO SULLY-SUR-LOIRE

Sweet, we'll slip away from them
(I hear the music of a band
Beyond the hill --
There may be a fair)
Your tender hand like a bird
Alive in my fingers
I will not look at you
I will not break the spell
(I will not need to look
Each particle of you
Is pressed upon my memory
Has left its outline there
For my quick blood to fill)
If this is a dream
Then there will be a village inn
Around this corner
With vestal roses by a whitewashed gate
Tables on a sunny terrace
Bright rooms with curtains
Blowing in the welcome breeze
And pillows for your splendid hair.

A LOVE SONG FOR
MIDSUMMER

Tramp out a bed
In head-
High corn
Where the air
Is full
Of ripening

Spread
Your hair
Like silk sheets
Everywhere

Call down
The birds
For wedding guests
Let the lark
Sing and the
Sparrow dance

And let
The stately crow
Witness
Our coupling
Warm
unhurried
apropos.

A LOVE SONG FOR
ST. VALENTINE'S DAY

I remember
that the gum
on the flap
of your envelope
was sweet

Once, careless,
I cut my tongue
licking it

The blood
on the side of my hand
was warm
and red as a heart.

A LOVE SONG FOR APRIL
OR THE FIRST WARM RAIN

I have to whisper it
The first warm rain reminds me of you
Not there, not there,
Then in a pose or word or gathering of light
Everywhere
And in that instant all in all
The air smells of your smell
The grass reaches up to touch you
What can I do?
I open up
To drink you in.

A LOVE SONG FOR THE CUSP OF FALL

You couldn't tell it from the slant of light
Or strands of cloud the northeast wind blew down
Across the bright brow of the morning

But as you made your matins
There in the pink haze of your bath
The sweet steam of your ablutions

Outside the sun was falling past the equinox
Its point of most precipitate decline
Where the curve flirts with the vertical
And this years no one's taking bets
On whether it will bounce again.

There's but cold comfort in imagining
The nadir's curl, the mirror of the minimum
Winking through the gray depth of December.

I'll take you for my pole and stay
And rig to bear the buffeting
With you my still, enduring love
Safe haven as the winter comes.

A LOVE SONG FOR THE
WINTER SOLSTICE

The wind's in the North quartering West
It sails a piece of yellow rag across the frozen lake
And out of sight. The other skaters, red and blue,
    are gone.
The glyphs they left show that they danced
Like dervishes, round and around. . . .

Now nothing moves here of its own accord
Not in the faceless sky or on the white land
Only a wisp of your hair waves in the wind.

Fine nerves could feel the trout turn underneath the ice
Fine eyes could see the shadows lengthen toward night
Fine balance sense the Earth coming about, its tiller
    hard alee. . . .

Be thou my weatherglass, my only love
And read out auguries of warm blue seas.

OLD MEN IN SPRINGTIME

Old men who walk the streets as yellow sun
Is rising into April and green grass
Divides the sidewalks and bright red
Tins and fire trucks and traffic lights
Gleam in the morning know more Spring
Then fifty poets; so do kids who shed
Their winter coats at recess, dropping them
Red green and yellow on the asphalt ground,
Omens of crocus and tulip that will come
Before we know it, you and I, who see
The Spring from autos, office windows, bars,
As time we speed through, one more obstacle
Between ourselves and where we have to go,
Or like a city from an airplane, lit
Green, red and yellow in the evening haze,
Gorgeous in its way, but far below.

IN THE ORCHARD

The trees must be
Pieces in some game
Very slow, so slow
Here a corner cut off
Here a crooked row
But on a field the same
As men in order
Holding their rocky ground

In the lanes among them there come ghosts
At evening, letting their white sheets unfold
Until they curl in the wind like fog
Left holding nothing, sinking on the trees like frost
A woman spirit and a man
Shameless and without guile . . .
She plays the pursued with elfin grace
Turning at last to face him when he's won
Back to a tree, embracing, sinking down

O the breath of love --
Clear and very soft, as soft
As the breath of a serpent
Sliding towards them through the broken grass.

HOLDING ON IN A HOWLING WIND

Today there's wind that comes from everywhere
    at once
Scratching at the tin roof
Kicking up the dust in the corral
Whipping a Wonder Bread wrapper from the trash
Miles off toward the willows at the bend
Where we'll find it months from now
And take it as an artifact of head high floods
Hung out to dry, red white and blue
Saying bodies can be built so many ways

But Spring will bring all that around
For now there someone's Stetson hat
Making for Texas like a frostbit duck
And there he runs off after it
(Or maybe he's in flight himself
Swimming in that wind like a scarecrow
His arms like windmill blades
The range grass raging at his feet like surf
The plains slate gray behind him
Flat and deep.)

DEATH AND THE WOMEN'S SODALITY

We watched him in his sickroom those last days
Having it out with death
Sucking breath through Teflon piping from a sighing
    pump
His eyes shut, pale with the intensity of his work;
Such dying was a thing we recognized from war
And there was honor in his going down.

Then to see him in the parlor of the funeral home
With Christian Muzak softly played
And the chat of older women and their fragrance
Mixing in the chaste and well-bred air
And to be guided by a gentle, white-gloved hand
Down the aisle into the blond-oak pew
To hear a service from the book of common prayer
By a well-groomed priest who knew him not at all

And then to see him lowered down
With flowers properly arranged
To lie in silence in his suit and tie
Ready to meet the ladies later, dignified
His fingernails immaculate, his every hair in place . . . .

I fear that in a room not far away
A matron with softly shadowed eyes
Wearing wide pink-tinted spectacles
Is unfolding chairs and setting them in rows

Seeing to the napkins and the cakes
Moving a table over by the door
Unfolding the roster of our names
Ready to greet us as we drop in, one by one.

DENOUEMENT AND EPILOGUE

My children bear me on through dumb shows of
despair
Dishevelled rooms, domestic carnage of machines
    that shudder and fail
Their fluids pooling on the dun concrete in the
    twenty-watt shade
Ankle deep and rising, threatening the clocks, the
    telephones, the radio . . .

In single file, my daughters and my son
The rods light on their supple shoulders, bear my
    ravaged weight
My box all red and gilt, and richly monogrammed

I am content with that which grieves my heart

Yet but a while and us the all-beholding sun shall see
    no more
Peace shall fall softly on these rooms
Once more in order all the brute machines await a
    word or human touch
My children regnant, solemn and unawed
I by then ashes scattered in the air
Casting the merest shadow on the concrete, left
As a faint grey stratum on the ground of being
For my heirs to read this little life from
And be staid.

WHAT WE WANT TO KNOW
ABOUT BEAUTY

What we want is the seeming, the wrapping, the face;
The perfect line of landscape
From peak to peak that
Comes from broken stone
We cannot see, just as
The dancer's perfect line of leg
From point to hip comes up
From hidden toes so calloused they can't flex,
And the perfect line of
Poetry comes out
Of midnights drunk with forcing words
To bend and bend until they all at once
Sing with the desperate grace of common things.

MERLIN OLD

It is my failing eyes, no doubt
That furnish the dark spaces of my cave
With figures of companions long since dead
So faint they vanish if I try to make them out;
My eyes that blur the edges of my field of view
So what I know at any given hour
Fades gently into what I must not think about.

The spirit voices that were once so strong
Tease me with rustlings, murmurings
That must be words but disappear
Before I catch them; and the song
I've always carried in my head,
The harmony of world and world to come,
Has come untuned, its rhythm broken, wrong . . . .

You need a certain grace to leave
Before you must, before they come to you
And say, their eyes downcast, "Perhaps
It would be better if . . . ."

And after all it is a tiring thing

The foolish posturing that keeps them sure

The powers are intact that once amazed.

I twist in my uncertainty; the glass

Reflects a passing spirit, free to go . . .

Besides that, only room and empty air.

And vague, vague shadows of what once was there.

AFTER THE SNOWSTORM

The children outside playing in the snow
Don't think of death, but I, inside
And warm and watching, think of little else;
The dark that's waiting past the afternoon
The cold to come, the kind that kills
Even the buried seeds, the wind that cries
And breaks the ice-encrusted trees
And creeps below the door into our house.

Once in Puerto Rico in a storm
I was a swimmer swept to sea
By rip tides; I have felt the force
Of the truth of things, and know
I cannot win by fighting back.

Then, I lived by letting go
By waiting out the sweep and swimming in
Because I knew that tide would turn.

In my house there are four clocks
And all of them agree that afternoon
Is soon to end. Too like the tide,
The dark swells out there to the east
And will inundate everything.

This time I know I can't let go.
My crippled heart would let go too,

And all my self simply give in
To wrap itself in whatever warmth remains
And sleep at last till I slept no more.

So it's in self-defense I write to you,
The offspring of the seeds that lived,
The holders of the heat your mom and I
Stirred up so long ago, trying to build
In spelling out my fears a barricade
Against oblivion.

I love you and I wish you well; you know
It's by your presence that I'll hold
A place, however tenuous,
In what's to come beyond the storm.

STAGING

Today the woman comes to stage my house.
I know her; my girl and hers were friends
And teammates. I recall their young blonde heads
Together on the bench, as we sat in our chairs
Behind them, watching softball games unfold.

Now, still blonde, she nears the open door
Where my agent, also blonde, awaits
Her clipboard at the ready.

                                    I have been
Through this before, and know the drill: get rid
Of everything that's not tied down,
From kitchen through to bathrooms.
Make the space look big by emptying.

I want to tell them about emptiness
More than they want to know, more than
Business conversations allow.
It is as if I have to hold my breath
To keep it in.

                           I studied how to breathe
In meditation class, beside my wife,
In rooms emptied of all distracting things.
Just mats, four others, and ourselves,
Five frightened pupils and a man who led
As we struggled to breathe through fear and pain.
I could not learn, but she did well enough

That at the end I was the one who gasped,
Who choked with fear as her poor heart gave out
Exhausted by the chemo, or just tired
Of keeping up the sad pretense of hope.

That other staging happened in a room
In diagnostic radiology.
Stage four, the doctor told her, after he
Insisted that we sit. I held her hand
And felt it clench, turn cold, then limply fall
Away from mine as if to say not even I
Could follow on this sudden fearful voyage.

And after that came drugs and distancing,
Falling away from town and house and room
And family until her world was bed,
Clear bags of dripping medicine, and sleep
And faces hovering, unrecognized.

Until the day the mask was taken off,
The futile drugs withdrawn, the curtains wide
To let her last Spring sunshine light her face.
Free from the fog of drugs and far past pain
She knew us at the last again; her eyes
Were clear, her lips formed words perhaps of love
And smiled just as the rush of last breath came
And she lay still, in light, emptied of everything.
And then, of course, the practicalities:
The calls, the paperwork, the turning out
Of drawers and closets, sorting what must go

To whom, and what might stay a while, the stage
Of dying no one talks about, the time
When busyness staves off the grief a while,
Until perhaps it's driven underground,
And what is left is absence.

                                              So I'd say
To these nice women who have come to help
If I could trust myself to talk without
Crying about the space I want filled up again
With all it was to live, this space, my home
That must be cleared now, must be subtly staged,
So buyers want it without knowing why.

THREE POEMS ON THE BEATITUDES

1. The Meek, Foregathered in the Lawyer's Office, Await the Reading of the Will

Not one among them dares to speak;
A gentle shuffling and the subtle creak of wooden
    chairs
Must bear the weight of making their impatience
    known.
Ten o'clock chimes out.
The final tone hangs in the breathless air.

Not one can quite discern whether the heavy door
Has moved a fraction of an inch;
No more can any hear a footfall on the floor beyond.

Perfect suspense grips all of them,
Their expectations poised against
What each has learned in life:
Who dares to reach beyond himself is doomed to
    fail and fall.

Somewhere, on another floor perhaps,
A tall solicitor regards the clock,
Checks the documents,
And thinks of starting toward the room
Of meek folks meekly waiting for their doom,

But, standing, pauses to regard the Earth
Outside his window, infinite of worth
Commended for safekeeping out of Grace
To those who'll stay in their appointed place.

2. Mourners Leaving the Cemetery by the Highway Gate

The rite is ended; the rabbi turns away
Closing his book. The family, all three,
Are folded into limos and are gone.
The mourners now turn grimly from their task,
Fourteen of them,
A chorus in grey skirts and overcoats
Black stockings, ties, the gentlemen in hats
The ladies veiled – by that they save the time
Of making eyes up – very much in line
With what is called for.

Across the highway from the grave
A pub gapes open like an empty mouth
To swallow all of them. From here,
It seems they're in a fair way to be comforted,
If not for long, then with intensity
By whiskey and their normal fees.

3: Those Who Hunger and Thirst for Righteousness Are Counseled About How Waters Actually Roll Down

When the waters come, you see, we all
Will be astounded at the force of them, just pouring
     down,
Just washing everything before them, all the raw
Detritus of a world so arid, so bereft of faith
So long there's nothing in it better than the bones
Of what was long ago, all the plastic scum
Of lethal food and drink, the filthy oil
Of progress, all the tinfoil parts
That made the engines turn, all, all
Come boiling down the canyons
On the flood of justice, rising fast
Through doomed cities, chipping loose
The whores and gamblers, cheats and thieves
The painted props of culture
The vacant leaders of all sorts and kinds
Bearing the walls of civic sham and
Monuments of vanity away,

                      and all you hopeful ones
Will be among them, for all your pleas;
The bodies of you thirsty hungry scattered in the
     aftermath
Athwart those of the less tuned in . . . my God
No one is righteous, no, not one, and judgment day

Will find you full, for sure – your guts and lungs
Sodden with justice, stuffed with muddy truth,
And your addled brains at last empty of pride.

THE COLONEL'S RESPONSE
TO THE CHAPLAIN

You charge me to say
How my job sorts with what you do.
I have no need to hold
Soldiering any closer
To my heart than the church
And all its intrigues
Are to yours. It is a thing
We must have; I do not
Pretend to know why.

Perhaps the question
After all is not
Why but why not --
I have read books
A thousand pages long
Struggling to unravel
Mysteries: why war?
Why plague? Why broken souls?

I have seen institutions rise
And fall, and lives come down
To shuddering last breaths
And cries for mercy,
And I have looked at Christ
Calm and inviting
Asking for the children to come

And I have put the question
To Him, and for answer had
The same inviting smile

I take it that "to be
As little children" means
To stop asking and do
As we are told. And so
I say again: the question is
Why not? It is the same

Question the cardinal asks
Considering a Cadillac,
The same God asked himself
Playing that game
Of pitch and toss with Satan
Over Job.

A soldier's life was good for me,
Despite the intervals of combat
The terror and the pain;
I learned to hold strength
In reserve for crises,
To let life happen as it will
In the easy days between.
If I must die tomorrow, I may hope
To take my going out with grace
As no more my affair, and no less just
Than was my coming in.

It was Jonathan Edwards
I believe, who put the larger
Question so: do not ask
Why God would cast souls down to hell;
Rather ask why not,
What forbearance or what whim
Would stay his hand?

I am a simple man
Not given to complexities.
You charge me that I justify my work.
I am not certain (please recall
That Christ also had doubts)
That what I do is right; I trust,
Without reason but with heart,
That my job must be done.

We do agree, your church and I
That mortals have no hope but grace,
That each of us, alone, corrupt,
Is powerless before the throne
Of judgment, abject and lost.

When I must look into the eyes
Of mothers whose sons I have myself
Sent into hell, I think of this:
I am the agent of a general

And he the agent of a government
Which is the agent of those mothers

And their sons, and all of us
And you, sir, too, agents
And victims of a providence
Beyond our power to know.

God has ordained, by precept
And by deed, that wars will be;
And my skill in them
Must be your hope for now; think of Job
In trouble. Pray.
Be strong.

OCCASIONAL SELF-ANALYSIS

-- homage to Karen Horney

Dear God, I am
A corner bar in a changing neighborhood
On some midwestern city's near southside,
My old German drunks such fixtures I could set the
    clock
By their getting up to piss, their seventh cigarettes;
Outside, through plate glass smoked like old-world fish
Tattered with colored flyers from a generation back
(Announcing the neighborhood events
Whose fading images collect in frames behind the bar,
Flocks of stocky women, working men
Whose names no longer matter, even here)
Through these windows, I say.
These windows out of me, I watch
The corner turning dark, the jive
Of streetwise kids who wait it out
In bus stop shelters, selling crack
Trading pussy for what feels so good
No German would admit it ever was . . .

Oh my dear God, I am trapped in here
What grim spell might free me I don't know
Nor where I'd go if suddenly the door
Swung open and those sudden kids
Their knit caps tilted back on their shaved heads
Entered like a jury of our peers
Appraising the querulous lot of us
A verdict forming in their narrow eyes.

SNAPSHOTS FROM
MY FAMILY ALBUM

My Father Fishing, 1939

My father holds the flyrod right, at one o'clock
Floating a popping bug across a shaded pool
Waist deep in the Ouachita west of Little Rock
In August water, gold and slow

On the gravel bar behind him, on a blanket
By an open picnic hamper, that is me
Just ten or fifteen pounds of suckling possibility
No trouble for him yet
And that is Mother with her thin shy smile

The thing that scares you is how young he is
And how unruffled, with his liquid eyes
His ruthless hand light on the rod
Still, waiting for the fish to rise.

Swimming in Lake Catherine, about 1950

Sometimes a camera overlooks important things.
You see the water, low, the bank of weeds pressed
    down,
Dry mud below it, and the bare bright wood
Of dock and diving board in stark noon light.
Hot weather, then; yet still this photo missed
The weight of thick mid-August Southern air
Wet as the stock-still standing lake itself.
Nor could it show the rancor baked into
The studied poses of these awkward boys
Waiting for girls who just don't seem to come
In time to catch their act. Yes, that is me,
There on the left, my brother by the rail,
Our cousin clowning on the diving board.
Don't let the smiles confuse you; we are ripe
For riot, set to go to foreign wars
With pleasure if that means we can escape
This inert countryside, this Southern grave
Of listless water and unyielding sun
Where there's no end to what cannot be done.

Uncle Herman, The Rake, about 1948

Uncle Herman stands in the wide side yard
Gallused, white shirted, in his good straw hat
His hand rests on the fender of his Chevrolet
A perfect husband's gesture: tender, masterly.

On the stoop behind him stand his mother and his aunt
Aproned and myopic, squinting at the sun
Good country women with their folded hands.
They are a chorus called out by surprise
Not sure which play this is, but happy to take parts.

On the hard grass in the near foreground
A skirted shadow points toward afternoon
Holding a shadow camera. This is all we have
Of the fourth or fifth young woman Herman loved
That summer, in that car, in Dardanelle.

Santa's Magic Kingdom at the Mall, December 30, 2023

Here is the Christmas Candy Court
Being unmagicked;
Peppermint pillars
Stone by pasteboard stone
Brought down and stacked;
The larger sugar plums
Black-plastic-bagged,
The smaller ones tossed into bins;
The white marshmallow Santa-throne
Upturned, de-legged,
And ready to be hauled away.

It's early yet; only a few
Mall walkers stop to watch.
They've seen this all before:
The build up in November
Then the rush, the climax
This dismantling.
They've been around, these folks;
They know the plot.

But still I like the look in that one's eyes
The smaller woman in the gray track suit –
I hope she's laughing inwardly
At how the take-down and the put-away
Are part of something, like the phony elves

And plastic sugar plums themselves,
So real that reason will not cope with it,
So natural it slips away from light
And finds a corner of the mind to settle in,
An ancient inglenook, from whence
It whispers legends to our eager hearts.

Myself at Seven in 1944

The point is not that this child's face --
This round white face whose narrowed eyes
Drill to the looker's core --
Has, transmogrified, become my own,
But that here's this happy birthday boy
Wearing his Tom Mix hat and chaps
With cheap tin cap guns in his hands
His legs athwart a hobby horse
Ready to shoot down anything that moves.

That's how we were in those days
A fact my mother (she's the shadow there
Indulging a young man's whim, as women do)
Knew all too well, and one my absent Dad
Whose home was in a foxhole at the time
Had reasons of his own to contemplate and rue.

C. B. Washburn Takes the Hand of
Emma Ethyl Cook, April 1887

Ten young men gather round the groom
Bareheaded, bearded, collarless
Impatient with the pose;
A rifle leans against the slanting porch.
Their shoes are mudcaked on the raw gray yard.

The women too go hatless.
Their braids are tight, after the German mode.
Only the bride wears jewelry;
A tiny cameo does up her blouse
His gift, and all she can expect.

The shade is sharp; it is a noon of early spring.
The cabin door leads in to empty space
Already Mother quickens in this bride child's womb
And Grandpa stares at generations yet to come
His eyes hard as the rifle steel
The future bare before him and downhill.

Aunt Ruth as a Bride in Little Rock, in 1933

Her man has brought her on the trolley car
She waits where he has led her, peering in
His breath is hard behind her in the hall

The door stands open to the bridal bed
Unmade, there by the bureau with the coal oil lamp
Next Monday she will be sixteen

Her pasteboard grip is bound up with his extra belt
Her handbag, stuffed with treasures brought from
    Dardanelle
(A child's things: buttons, postcards, trinkets made
    of glass)
Hangs from her elbow. Her long wool skirt is fringed
    with dust.
Still as a doe she notes the land that's hers

Her mouth is calm, as calm as it will be
Six decades later, on the day she dies
But something sterner clings like soot
In the hollows of her young and wizened eyes.

Aunt Cravens in her Memphis Dress, 1958

This is Aunt Cravens in the old folks home
In nineteen fifty-eight or so
Her hair just done, her glasses on
A trace of color on her cheeks and lips

This scarlet, flowered dress will be her shroud;
She wears it every Sunday, as she has
Since Uncle Wallace died in forty-six
And left her eighty, sole, and all but penniless.

She went to Memphis for it, by herself
Driving his Buick though she couldn't see
Above the steering wheel, three hours there
Three hours back, without a qualm;

She paid more for it than she paid for him
To be laid out, and wore it to the funeral
To shock her stolid children and the town
Claiming her right to live beyond her grief

Here, bent and whiskered, ninety-two years old
She smiles for visitors and lets them know
She's dressed up for the hell of it
Albeit there's no place left to go.

Uncle Dieter in the Idle Hour, in 1949

What does life cost besides the things
One parts with willingly?
This gaunt, tall man holds out his stein
(The ornate one he brought with him
From the Rheinland to the middle west
With one drab suit, some underwear
And Aunt Mathilde's down-filled comforter)
Asking this of any one at all
Who'll sit down long enough to crack
His thick-tongued gutterals
And tell him why, when life's so short
No one sings drinking songs in Dardanelle
And Baptists on the corner lurk to count
His visits to this filthy bar
Where slack-jawed strangers belt it back
In hostile silence, and the smells
Of piss and pigs' feet mix with greasy light
In brutal mocking of gemuetlichkeit.

My Son and a Friend on the Road in Texas, 1987

The plane of desert leads the eye away
To nothing more specific than some mare's-tail clouds
The only sign of moisture anywhere --
Save a point where a water drop, or sweat
Has dulled the finish of the print --
Nor is there motion; nothing blurs
All seems in balance.
By the asphalt, by a sign announcing State Road 88
Two fugitives lean inward toward each other's arms
Their packs beside them in the dust.
His shirt is out, his jeans torn at the knees
His ball cap pools his face in shade down to his grin;
His teeth in sunlight glow like weathered bone
The whitest thing for fifty miles around.
And the companion, who must be a she
By length of braids and softening of chin
Smiles, but narrowly and with closed lips;
Her head's inclined as if she's listening
To distant water or such wind
As drives the mare's tails down the sky
And there's a tension in her neck and jaw
That tells she's not enchanted with New Mexico
The edge of which is poised just out of sight
Beyond the rough horizon, or perhaps
Is angry with the third and unknown traveller
Whose camera carves this figure of her flight.
Way behind them, hard to read against the sage

A second sign urges the gist of things:
NO STOPPING OR STANDING.
In Texas, they will learn, and everywhere,
Their time flows by them like the mare's tail wind
Like water absent for ten million years but coming back
And though they loiter, yet they make their way
By seas and deserts interleaved and one
Toward the ultimate and sad surprise
That dooms their dream of staying for a while
In Texas, or New Mexico, or paradise.

Cousin Buddy and His Mother, about 1932

The elms are saplings in this shot;
Fourteenth Street's curbed but not yet paved --
Behind the house the shadow of the barn that was
Clings to the whitewashed fence. On the porch in front
A gathering; neighbors, friends
And family. It might be Labor Day
Or just a pleasant Sunday afternoon for paying calls.

That's Cousin Buddy in the overalls
Smiling his squinty smile; just from the way
He holds his hands up, like a girl defends
Her handbag, you can see he's odd, or to be blunt
Retarded. That's his father on the swing. His ma's
The somber one, upright and gaunt, who's saved
Only the hulking child whom she begot.

Her eyes are pregnant with what can't be said:
She loves this boy, and wishes he were dead.

My Children in Mid December, 1982

This is the old house, and its living room
Of paneled walls, tall windows opening
Upon wide yard and wider woods beyond
All white with rare December snow, where elms
Raise up their thin black arms in mock surprise.
Among them scattered junipers, as round
As spools of warm green yarn. It's one of these
That stands now in the corner of this room.
The children, having covered it with chains
Of paper, lights, and bright glass ornaments
Repose like heroes on the couch and floor.
They've left to me the angel that must go
On top of everything, where only I
Can reach; except for that small, vital task
I am irrelevant. This ample room
Gives all they need of walls against the cold
That peers in darkly from the winter woods;
The tree gives all they need of saving grace.
They do not think of what it takes to keep
The wan world outside while they watch or sleep.

Uncle Tony With a Bust of Voltaire

Sad, dark draped image, this
Some itinerant photographer's
Idea of classic art, but Uncle T
Is obviously uncomfortable
In high white collar and cravat;
His hand, mechanic's grime indelible
Around the nails, lies still
Upon the table where the bust
Speaks to the vanity of its age
And ours: Tout pour le meilleur, indeed . . .

Aunt Una's portrait hangs just out of sight
Behind him, watching with calm common sense
His shame, the fear that makes his forearm tense;
Perhaps the sweat is beading on his temples now
But he's a man; he'll hold the pose somehow;
With might and main, he means to make things right.

Mother in Flight, 1932

Here is my mother sailing through the air
Her back arched perfectly, her hands flung wide
From two young men who have tossed her up
To one who waits to pull her down.

Her skirt is longer than skirts are these days
It scarcely leaves her ankles bare;
Her hair is bobbed, her eyes are large
Her lips are small and bowed, and in her smile
Is a pretty hint of fear of flight.

Behind this act the others make a pyramid
And one girl yells into a megaphone.

Still farther back the crowded stands
Are freighted with the people of the day.
Lost in that blur my father cheers
Some progress on the football field
Anonymous, not having met her yet,
Happy among his friends and raising hell,
Hardly guessing while the game goes on
That this young and frightened bird
Will make his life-mate, pair with him
To fly for sixty years and more
Through calm air and otherwise
Farther than their fledgling selves could dream.

Aunt Gladys at Home in Dardanelle, about 1950

Bone china brought from Memphis back before the War
Crystal, linen, silver condiments
Soberly arrayed, on center, lustrous in the indoor light
Sieved through curtains laced like angels' wings
These are the tokens of the widow's trade
She is its mistress, and the mistress of this house.

The girl beside her is the parlor maid
Behind them by the flawless mirror there's a trace
Of motion, as if something had been caught
In flight; the kitchen help, perhaps
Or maybe just her husband's ghost
A harmless haunt in these stout walls, built with his nails
And timber he hauled down by wagon from Crow Hill

But ghost or no ghost, there she stands
Her bosom boned, her hair done up
Her waist at sixty still a mere hand's span
For men his size, thinking perhaps
Of how he held her there, and shook the chandelier
His teeth like china through his ruddy beard
Or how her breasts came free in his rough hands
Before the strain of building took him off
And left her with all this to call her own
To do with as the circumstance demands.

Uncle Hans in Oklahoma, Winter, 1917

A year ago he scaled the Zugspitze
In shorts, a sweater, hiking boots
Ganz stolz, a master of the ice
A spider on the rock face
When luck turned bad and rotten stone
Rattled down to doom beneath his feet
He kept ascending, looked no way but up
Rose like a bird, bouyed by the alpine air
Then made his way down to Alberstal
To read his mail: the war had found him out.
He left his home that night with what he wore
And hiked the forty miles to Switzerland.

By Muskogee in the winter there is wind
Whistling in the fields that sang the same song
Yesterday in Yellow Knife, come from the pole
Unfenced. In it he stands to pose.
Behind him is no mountain but a spindly barn
Sagging under half a foot of snow
Where six gaunt heifers face into the draft
And chickens peck among their steaming dung.
He bears a hayfork bravely, like a gun.
The cold soaks through his ragged coat
It is near zero in the afternoon
His eyes are raised toward the basalt sky
But there's no purchase;
In the dead flat farm we read his fate:
There they wait to kill him
Here he can't move, up or down.

**Aunt Emmeline and Uncle Dodger
in Fair Park, about 1958.**

59

The shade of oaks half hides her face
But see how slim she is, and fair
And graceful, in her summer lace
With satin ribbons in her hair . . .

Her husband's simple visage bares
His soul; his dark uncertain frown
Confronts the camera which dares
To steal her image, set her down

A shadow on some album page
Which might be touched, which might be found
Attractive; might somehow engage
Emotions, give some rival ground

For thinking she's available.
He'll not have that; his massive arm
Surrounds her, unassailable;
She sits unsmiling, safe from harm.

Bob Boyd is a retired teacher and free-lance journalist whose work has appeared in *The Nation*, the Chicago Tribune, the Los Angeles Times, and regularly from 1968 through the 1990s in the *St. Louis Post-Dispatch*. His stories and poems have appeared in *Southern Poetry Review*, *Confrontation*, *The Greensboro Review*, *River Styx*, *Webster Review*, *Chariton Review*, and elsewhere. He has won the Guy Owen Prize and the Missouri Writers' Week award for poetry. His novel, *Cohea's Tower*, and a book of his stories, *Family Values*, have been published by Yettie Publishing, St. Louis.

This project was made possible, in part, by generous support from the Osage Arts Community.

Osage Arts Community provides temporary time, space and support for the creation of new artistic works in a retreat format, serving creative people of all kinds — visual artists, composers, poets, fiction and nonfiction writers. Located on a 152-acre farm in an isolated rural mountainside setting in Central Missouri and bordered by ¾ of a mile of the Gasconade River, OAC provides residencies to those working alone, as well as welcoming collaborative teams, offering living space and workspace in a country environment to emerging and mid-career artists. For more information, visit us at www.osageac.org